PEOPLE WHO HELP US

Flight Attendant

Alison Cooper and Diana Bentley

Photographs by
Chris Fairclough

Wayland

People Who Help Us

Ambulance Crew
Bus Driver
Firefighter
Flight Attendant
Lifeboat Crew
Nurse
Police Officer
Train Driver
Vet

Designer: David Armitage

First published in 1990 by
Wayland (Publishers) Ltd
61 Western Road, Hove
East Sussex, BN3 1JD, England

© Copyright 1990 Wayland (Publishers) Ltd

British Library Cataloguing in Publication Data
Cooper, Alison
    Flight attendant.
    1. Air transport passenger services. Stewards
    I. Title II. Bentley, Diana III. Series
    387.742

    ISBN 1–85210–982–3

Typeset by Nicola Taylor, Wayland
Printed and bound in Belgium by Casterman S.A.

Contents

Words that are <u>underlined</u> appear
in the glossary on page 30.

Have you ever been to an airport?

You might have visited an airport to watch the aeroplanes taking off and landing. Perhaps you have been to an airport to go on holiday. People can travel all over the world by aeroplane.

Simon is a <u>flight attendant</u>.

Simon looks after people who are travelling by aeroplane. He makes sure that they are safe and comfortable during their flight.

Simon starts work at the airport.

Simon works at Gatwick airport, near London. All the people who work at the airport have a <u>pass</u>. Simon shows his pass to the <u>security guard</u>. The guard opens the <u>barrier</u> for Simon.

Simon tells Dawn that he is working on the flight to the Canary Islands. She crosses his name off her list. She has to make sure that all the flight attendants have arrived for their flights.

Simon goes to a meeting with the flight attendants who are working with him today. They have to know what to do if there is an accident, or if a passenger is ill.

The flight attendants get on to a bus. It takes them to the aeroplane.

The passengers are waiting for their flight.

The passengers check in for their flight here. The people at the desks tell them where they will be sitting on the aeroplane. The passengers' baggage is taken to be loaded into the aeroplane's <u>hold</u>.

Rebecca and Malcolm are going to the Canary Islands for their holiday. They are very excited. They wait in the departure lounge with their mum and dad until it is time for them to get on to the aeroplane.

Simon is on the aeroplane.

The flight attendants check the <u>passenger cabin</u> before the passengers arrive. They make sure that there are enough meals on the aeroplane for all the passengers. Simon checks that all the <u>fire extinguishers</u> are working properly.

Here are the pilots.

The pilots have checked all their <u>instruments</u>. Everything is working properly. When the passengers are on the aeroplane, the pilots will move it to the start of the runway, ready for take-off.

The passengers get on to the aeroplane.

The passengers travel on a bus from the airport buildings to the aeroplane. They climb up the steps.

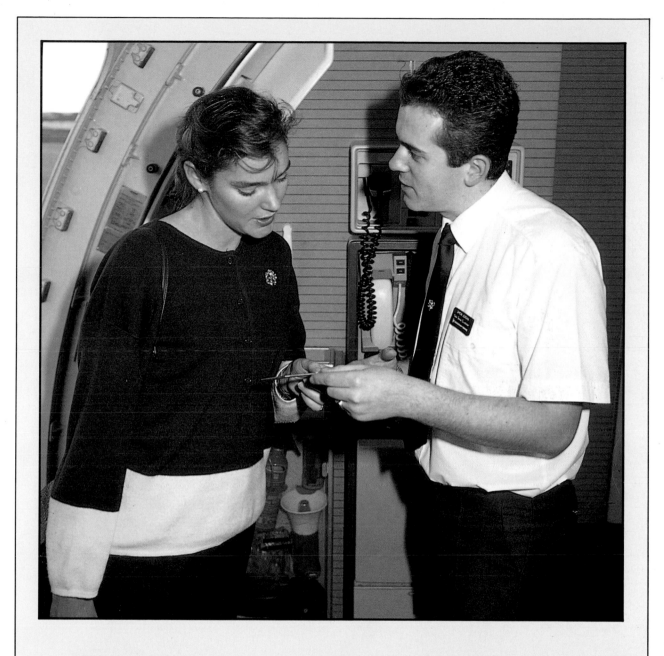

Simon is waiting for them at the top of the steps. He says hello to the passengers. He tells them where to find their seats.

The <u>cabin crew</u> get ready for take-off.

Simon shows the passengers where to put their bags while the aeroplane is taking off.

The cabin crew make sure that all the passengers know what to do if there is an accident. Simon shows them how to use a <u>life jacket</u>, in case the aeroplane has to come down in the sea.

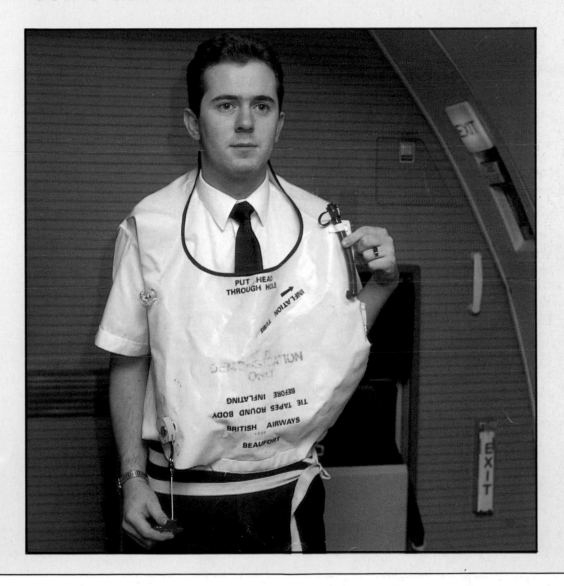

The aeroplane takes off.

All the passengers have fastened their seatbelts. Simon has to sit down during take-off. He fastens his seatbelt too. The aeroplane is speeding down the runway.

The aeroplane climbs into the sky. Soon it will be 10 km above the ground. The flight to the Canary Islands will take about four hours.

Simon looks after the passengers.

Simon helps Di to get the drinks ready. He takes them to the passengers in his section on a trolley.

Simon gives colouring books to the children. It is a long flight and he does not want them to get bored. What do you like to do on a long journey?

Simon is in the <u>galley</u>.

The meals are prepared at the airport. Then they are heated in the ovens on the aeroplane. There are over two hundred people in the cabin waiting for their dinner.

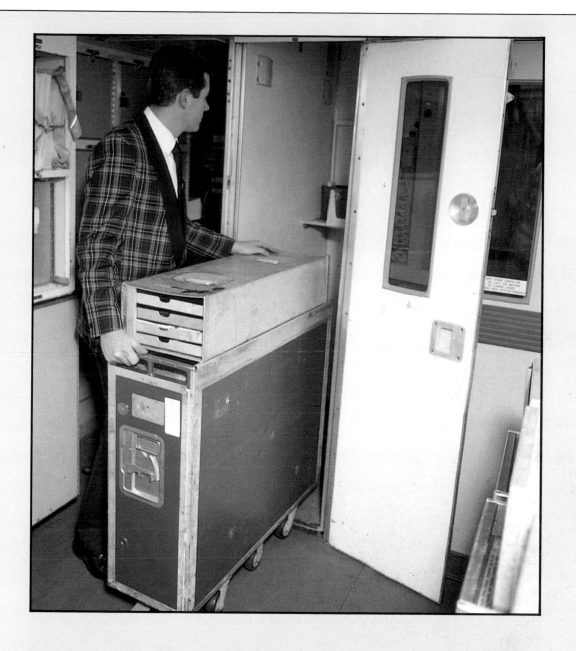

Simon puts the trays of food on to a trolley.
He puts the trolley in the lift and sends it up
to the passenger cabin.

The passengers are having their dinner.

Simon serves the meals to the passengers.
Rebecca and Malcolm enjoy their dinner.

The flight is almost over.

Simon and Di write a report. Some of the people on the flight needed special meals. Simon orders special meals for their flight home too.

Simon calls the galley. Some of the cabin crew are clearing away the meal trolleys. He tells them to come up to the cabin. It is time to get ready for landing.

Simon says goodbye.

The aeroplane has landed at the airport in the Canary Islands. Simon says goodbye to the passengers. He hopes that they will enjoy their holiday.

Glossary

<u>Barrier</u>   A gate across the entrance to a building, factory or car park.

<u>Cabin crew</u>   A group of flight attendants working together on an aeroplane.

<u>Check in</u>   Show their tickets.

<u>Fire extinguishers</u>   Containers that are full of water or foam. They are used to put out fires.

<u>Flight attendant</u>   Somebody who looks after people travelling on aeroplanes.

<u>Galley</u>   The kitchen on an aeroplane or ship.

<u>Hold</u>   The part of the aeroplane where the baggage is kept during the flight.

<u>Instruments</u>   Machines that help the pilots to fly the aeroplane.

<u>Life jacket</u>   A jacket without sleeves that is filled with air. It helps people to float in water.

<u>Pass</u>   A card that shows that the person who carries it may go into a particular building.

<u>Passenger cabin</u>   The part of the aeroplane where the passengers sit.

<u>Security guard</u>   A person who makes sure that everybody who enters a particular building has a pass.

Books to read

Airliners William Green and Gordon
   Swanborough (Frederick Warne, 1987)
Air Stewardess Anne Stewart (Hamish Hamilton,
   1984)
Going on a Plane Anne Civardi (Usborne, 1988)
Let's Look At Aircraft Andrew Langley (Wayland,
   1989)
My Visit to The Airport Sophie Davies and Diana
   Bentley (Wayland, 1989)

Acknowledgements

The authors and publishers would like to thank Caledonian
Airways for their help in the preparation of this book and, in
particular, the following people: Simon Jordan, Elaine Shepherd,
Lorraine Gillies, Madeline Pearson; the flight and cabin crews on
flights KT 486/487; Mr and Mrs Jones and family; Mr and Mrs
Cooper and family.

Index